# THE LONDON BOROUGH OF
# HACKNEY
## IN OLD PHOTOGRAPHS
### 1890–1960

A GENTLE SUMMER AFTERNOON BOATING on the Walthamstow reservoirs for one of the Hanbury family of Stainforth House, and best friend, c. 1900.

# THE LONDON BOROUGH OF
# HACKNEY
## IN OLD PHOTOGRAPHS
### 1890–1960

FROM HACKNEY ARCHIVES DEPARTMENT

COMPILED BY

# DAVID MANDER
# AND JENNY GOLDEN

ALAN SUTTON

Alan Sutton Publishing Limited
Phoenix Mill · Far Thrupp · Stroud · Gloucestershire

First published 1991

**British Library Cataloguing in Publication Data**

The London Borough of Hackney in old photographs.
I. Mander, David, *1953–*   II. Golden, Jenny
942.144

ISBN 0-86299-963-4

## DEDICATION
For Len and Margaret

Typeset in 9/10 Korinna.
Typesetting and origination by
Alan Sutton Publishing Limited.
Printed in Great Britain by
The Bath Press, Avon.

# CONTENTS

| | | |
|---|---|---|
| | INTRODUCTION AND STREET INDEX | 7 |
| 1. | THE VICTORIAN AND EDWARDIAN HOUSE AND GARDEN | 9 |
| 2. | THE CHANGING SCENE I | 17 |
| 3. | 'IT WILL ALL BE OVER BY CHRISTMAS': FIRST WORLD WAR | 25 |
| 4. | THE CHANGING SCENE II | 35 |
| 5. | SHOPS AND MARKETS | 51 |
| 6. | BUSINESS AND INDUSTRY | 61 |
| 7. | MORE LIGHT, MORE POWER: LOCAL GOVERNMENT | 69 |
| 8. | PUBLIC HEALTH AND HOUSING | 83 |
| 9. | POVERTY AND SICKNESS | 103 |
| 10. | GETTING ABOUT | 115 |
| 11. | KEEPING AMUSED | 121 |
| 12. | THE SPORTING LIFE | 133 |
| 13. | 'READ ALL ABOUT IT': POLITICS AND SPECIAL EVENTS | 139 |
| 14. | 'TAKE COVER': SECOND WORLD WAR | 145 |
| 15. | ACKNOWLEDGEMENTS | 160 |

PLANE TREES IN THE GROVE: looking north from the south-west corner towards Spurstowes Almshouses on the morning of 29 May 1900. The railings are at the back of the second Hackney Town Hall. Most of this site is now occupied by the present Town Hall.

# INTRODUCTION

It is pleasing to be able to follow up the first Hackney old photograph book with a second, taking the visual story of the area forward to the 1950s. There is a little overlap between the two volumes, as this one starts with the 1890s. This has allowed the inclusion of photographs that have come into Hackney Archives Department in the last two years as well as some that could not be fitted into the first book. This has filled some gaps in the collection; for instance we are now able to show streets in the De Beauvoir Town and Dalston areas before the First World War, and a selection from a postcard collection is included in this volume.

As in the previous book, the photographs are drawn from the Hackney Archives Department collection, which includes copies of material in other collections or kindly loaned to us. Rather than repeat the area format of the previous book, this one is arranged more as a social history and considerable space has been allowed for the two World Wars and the major upheavals caused by housing programmes between the wars. Inevitably, photographs are not always available to illustrate all events, but more are constantly coming to light and so those we have not been able to show here may be illustrated in a future volume.

The thematic approach has inevitably scattered views of the same location throughout the book, and so we have provided an index of street and estate names.

The last book drew on a relatively small number of photographers and it was possible to say something about them and their work. The twentieth century saw the dramatic growth of the postcard, and we have used many examples in this book from local and national series. Local authorities became more active in recording their areas, notably in medical services, slum clearance and, in Hackney's case, bomb damage. The local newspaper used few photographs in its columns, but in some cases we have drawn on national coverage of local events like the earthquake of 1931 or the riot outside the Brotherhood Church in 1917.

I would like to thank my collaborator, Jenny Golden, for her share of the selection, research and captions that have gone to make up the book. We hope that it will bring back a few memories and settle a few arguments as to what was where, and when.

David Mander
June 1991

# STREET INDEX

Albion Grove, 24, 25
Albion Square, 77
Amwell Court, 97
Austins Buildings, 98
Banister House, 88, 89
Banister Street, 100
Barn Street, 94
Brunswick Place, 130–1
Caroline Street, 94
Charles Square, 44
Charnwood House, 94
Chatham Place, 36
Chatsworth Road, 19, 24
Church Crescent, 151
Clapton Common, 50, 124, 133, 160
Clapton Passage, 159
Clarence Terrace, 98
Clissold Park, 29, 134
College Street, 88
Commercial Street, 126
Conduit Court, 89
Craven Lodge, 18
Cressett Street, 149
Dalston Lane, 19, 155
De Beauvoir Road, 21
Digby Road, 34
Downs Road, 52
Duncan Road, 91
Edred House, 101
Egerton Road, 22
Ettrick House, 94
Fairchild House, 99
Finsbury Avenue, 93
Forest Road Estate, 99
Fox Lane, 32
Frampton Park Road, 152
Fulham Place, 98
Gainsborough Road, 53, 59, 105
Gainsborough Square, 83
Goldsmith Row, 127
Graham Road, 20
Green Lanes, 49, 96
Greenwood Road, 9
Hackney Churchyard, 91
Hackney Grove, 6
Hackney Road, 43
Hackney Station, 119
Handley Road, 95
Heywood Buildings, 89
Hillcot House, 98
Holly Street, 21
Homerton High Street, 37, 88, 89, 103–5
Homerton Row, 88
Hoxton Market, 111–13
Hoxton Square, 120
Hoxton Street, 57, 65
Kenmure Road, 120
Kenninghall Road, 108
King Edward Road, 11–14
Kingsland High Street, 36, 39, 46, 56, 57
Kingsland Road, 60, 64–5, 102, 109, 118, 122
Kingsmead Estate, 101
Lauriston Road, 90
Lea Bridge Road, 38

Lea, River, 77, 136–7
Linscott Road, 152
Lockner Road, 102
Londesborough Road, 154
Lordship House, 97
Lordship Lane, 48
Lordship Road, 123
Lower Clapton Road, 39–40, 53, 58, 67, 79, 100, 106,    109, 116, 135
Mapledene Road, 20
Manor House, 117, 119
Mare Street, 22, 35, 51, 70–3, 82, 106, 129, 147, 150,    153, 154, 158
Mentmore Terrace, 150
Millfields Road, 85
Morning Lane, 52
Morningside Estate, 100
Nevill Road, 33
New North Road, 63
Nichols Square, 102
Nisbet Street, 98
Old Street, 59, 78
Otley Terrace, 88
Paradise Row, 18
Pear Tree Court, 98
Pitfield Estate, 99
Pitfield Street, 78, 81
Poole Street, 66
Powell House, 100
Princess May School, 28
Queensdown Road, 23
Queens Square, 93
Rendlesham Road, 10, 61
Regents Canal, 115
Richmond Road, 85
Ridley Road, 54
Ritson Road, 107
Rookwood, 23
Rossington Street, 94
St Thomas Square, 149
Shacklewell, 38
Shacklewell Lane, 90
Shore Road, 15
Southgate Road, 27
Springfield, 122
Spring Hill, 17, 68
Spring Lane, 90
Stamford Hill, 55, 118
Stoke Newington Church Street, 18, 26–7, 32, 34, 47,    49, 75, 79, 121, 148, 158
Stoke Newington High Street, 47, 58, 116
Stoke Newington Road, 46
Triangle, Mare Street, 22
Tresham Avenue, 158
Upper Clapton Road, 50, 55, 151
Valette Street, 96
Warnford Street, 60
Well Street, 54
Wetheral Road, 90
Weymouth Terrace, 45
Wick Road, 156, 157
Woodberry Down, 29
Woodberry Road, 48
Yorkton Street, 44

# The Victorian and Edwardian House and Garden

INFORMAL SCENES OF EDWARDIAN HOME LIFE are not common and most of the family views of Hackney before 1914 are formal groups, street scenes or events. Most of this section comes from one family, the Butters, whose links with the area began in 1848, when Charles Butters began to acquire land for development on lease from St Thomas's Hospital in South Hackney. Butters moved into one of his own houses, Parkfield Villa, 41 King Edward Road and his son Walter (1839–1906) lived two doors away at No. 45. The family stayed in the building business which was continued by a younger member, George, from nearby Warnford Street. The family were keen gardeners and amateur photographers. The view on this page is not their own work, but it would have amused them – the tempted dog is in the back garden of Dr Ebenezer Prout at 12 Greenwood Road, in 1896.

OUTDOOR PORTRAITS WERE EASIER THAN INDOOR ONES; here Mrs Eleanor Smith and her aspidistra are photographed gracing the back door of 119 Rendlesham Road, c. 1900.

THE FRONT OF WALTER BUTTERS'S HOUSE, 49 King Edward Road, c. 1900 and (below) the back garden in the summer of 1884 or '85 with (back row) Annie Offor, Walter and Charles Butters and (front row) Annie and Katie Butters.

A GLIMPSE INSIDE THE HOUSE: above is the sitting room, below Walter Butters sits in state surrounded by his walking-stick collection. Both views C. 1900.

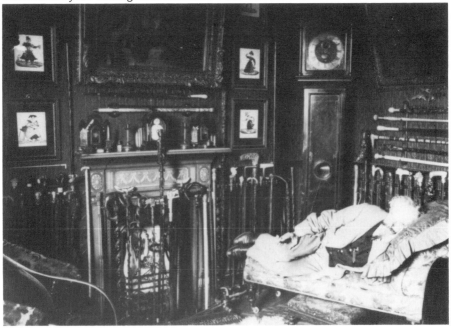

GARDEN LIFE included apple gathering as well as more restful pursuits. In the top view Anne Butters is on the ladder, with Walter looking up by the man with the hat. The elder Annie is holding a pole by the seated old lady. The swing group includes Walter (behind), Charles and Katie on the swing seat, Annie sewing and young Anne to her left. Both views date from around 1890.

GREAT FUN WAS HAD BY ALL. In the children's den are George (between the fire and the ladder), Frank (on the ladder) and Charles (by the hut). In front of the washing are Anne, Walter and Katie. Ten years later amateur dramatics were keeping Charles and Walter busy, as shown in this view taken by the garden stairs, c. 1900.

GEORGE BUTTERS later became a builder in the same area of South Hackney. This group taken in the garden of 19 Shore Road during the first decade of this century shows Kate and Martha with Leslie and Douglas and a very splendid rocking horse.

THE GRANGE AND STONELEIGH HOUSE, Paradise Row, at the west end of Stoke Newington Church Street, reflected in the New River, c. 1929. These were both demolished in 1936 by the LCC for the construction of flats now on the site. Inhabitants of the Grange included Egyptologist Samuel Sharpe (1799–1881). The loss of houses like this and the culverting of the New River in 1952 radically altered this end of Stoke Newington Church Street.

# The Changing Scene
## I

THE PERIOD 1890–1914 saw considerable change in the north of Hackney, with development completed and some of the middle classes moving out of the area. This is Spring Hill House, on the south side of Spring Hill, parts of which dated from the sixteenth century, though extensively remodelled in the late eighteenth and early nineteenth centuries. This view was taken in 1883, and it remained largely unchanged until 1904 when its last occupier, Thomas Garland, sold it for incorporation in the new Springfield Park. It was far from a compulsory purchase as Garland had been treasurer of the campaign to create the park!

CRAVEN LODGE in 1904, shortly before and during demolition. The house had been built in the early nineteenth century for John Craven (1757–1836). After being home to the philanthropist Samuel Morley from 1854 to 1870 it remained empty while its extensive estate, bounded by the present Craven Park Road, Stamford Hill and the River Lea, was gradually built over and its numerous ponds filled in.

BY CONTRAST THIS WAS BUSTLING DALSTON LANE from the junction with Beechwood Road looking west, about 1913. On the left is the Dalston Theatre, opened in 1886, converted to a cinema in 1922 and now the Four Aces Club. The Dalston Picture Palace was the briefest of competitors, only lasting from 1910 to 1914.

CHATSWORTH ROAD with market stalls, from the junction with Blurton Road looking north towards Rushmore Road School in 1905.

THIS IS TRAFFIC-FREE GRAHAM ROAD from the junction with Navarino Road, c. 1910. Although completed in 1872, Graham Road remained quiet but for the passing of trams and it was growth in road traffic in the 1950s that changed it for the worse.

MAPLEDENE ROAD, a view from opposite No. 53 looking east to Landsdowne Drive, from a postcard of about 1912. This portion of the road had been named Shrubland Grove until the previous year.

THE SOUTHERN END OF DE BEAUVOIR ROAD looking north to the Downham Road junction, also in 1912. These houses of the early 1840s were demolished for Hackney Council's De Beauvoir Town estate in the mid-1960s.

THE HOPE PUBLIC HOUSE and adjoining houses in Holly Street, looking north, c. 1912. This area was cleared in 1957–8 for the Holly Street Estate.

MORLEY HALL AND THE TRIANGLE, Mare Street, a view looking west, c. 1895. Named after the philanthropist Samuel Morley, the hall was acquired by trustees associated with Cambridge Heath Congregational Church after the original public company had failed during the hall's construction. Opened in 1879 it was the home of the Hackney and East Middlesex Band of Hope Union until 1924 and then became a factory. Bomb-damaged in the Second World War, the site is now part of Hackney College.

THE NEW SYNAGOGUE, on the south side of Egerton Road, was built on the Craven Park Estate and opened on 21 March 1915, when guests included Sir Marcus Samuel, the first Jewish Lord Mayor of London and Alderman Herbert Ormond, in his capacity of Mayor of Stoke Newington. This view dates from shortly after the opening.

THE ARK OF THE COVENANT, the Agapemonite church on Rookwood Road, seen here in 1906, twenty years after its construction as the first London church of the sect. In 1902 the new sect leader, Smyth Piggott, caused a sensation by proclaiming himself the new Messiah. Left empty in the mid-1920s, the church is now used by the Ancient Catholics.

THE EAST SIDE OF QUEENSDOWN ROAD and Hackney Downs, with Downs Baptist Church of 1869. Despite the claims of debauchery made by the minister of a local Presbyterian church, the Downs was a respectable place for a quiet walk and not a 'plague spot' with hundreds of couples lying about shamelessly on the grass.

ON THE VERGE OF WAR: volunteers of the Stoke Newington Battalion of the National Reserve lined up for inspection by army officers, including Field Marshal Sir John French and Stoke Newington Mayor Herbert Ormond, 25 July 1914.

ALSO ON THE VERGE OF WAR was Henry Lunkin's German bakery at 71 Chatsworth Road in 1913. On the outbreak of war the shop was looted in an anti-German riot on 6 August 1914, which may have been initiated by disgruntled tenants of Lunkin's who faced a rent rise. Many of Hackney's large German community faced violence or the threat of it in the first few months of the war.

# 'It will all be over by Christmas': First World War

'THE DIE IS CAST,' said the *Hackney Gazette* on 7 August 1914, and urged local mayors to convene meetings and committees to coordinate local responses. All three boroughs did so, though with different concerns. Shoreditch was worried by the problems of poor relief to dependants of volunteers and unemployment arising from curtailment of exports. Hackney had to face a brief outburst of anti-German feeling, while Stoke Newington, with a more prosperous population, diversified into volunteer effort at home. What Stoke Newington did in the war features strongly in this section, including our opening view of the prize-giving platform at the opening of the Volunteers headquarters, in Albion Grove, 25 July 1914. Besides French and Mayor Ormond, other luminaries include the architect W.F. Loveday and Stoke Newington's Town Clerk, George Willis.

HM LANDSHIP *Julian*, 'The Tank Bank', on a fund-raising visit to Stoke Newington Church Street on 16 March 1918. Organized by Mayor Herbert Ormond, seen orating on the top of the tank (above) the day included a lottery, band music and a rendering of Hearts of Oak, led from the tank top. The well-attended event raised £112,000 in war bonds.

HACKNEY AND STOKE NEWINGTON proposed establishing food kitchens; Stoke Newington opened one at 30 Stoke Newington Church Street in January 1918 and a second in St Matthias church hall, Wordsworth Road. Here Mayor Ormond is promoting delights ranging from soup at 1d. to sausages at 4d. to his young audience. Both kitchens closed in March 1919.

NOT EVERYONE WAS A FERVENT WAR SUPPORTER. The Brotherhood Church in Southgate Road saw several pacifist meetings where speakers included Sylvia Pankhurst. One meeting organized on 28 July 1917 by the communist-inspired London & Home Counties Workers and Soldiers Council led to a riot as crowds stormed the building, injuring some delegates.

LOCAL CEREMONIES EMPHASIZED OFFICIAL SUPPORT. Here a field ambulance is being dedicated on 31 December 1915 by the Bishop of London and other ministers in the yard of Princess May School.

DIGGING FOR VICTORY in Clissold Park as men of the Stoke Newington Vacant Lands Cultivation Society prepare to turn part of the park into allotments.

WOMEN WERE ALSO ENCOURAGED to support the war effort and were active on flag days. Here volunteers are working in the needle and slipper room of the Stoke Newington War Hospital Supply depot at 16 Woodberry Down. Founded in 1915, the depot remained active until the Armistice.

THE STOKE NEWINGTON VOLUNTEER BATTALION brought in a variety of training exercises before members were despatched to the front. This selection of views was mostly taken at the summer camp at Tadsworth, near Epsom in 1917. In May of that year the Battalion had taken part in an exercise in defence of that great German strategic objective, Chingford, and the commander, Major E.H. Coumbe exhorted his troops to hold on to High Beech at all costs. Even at the beginning of the war a local paper had reported that the volunteers were making tremendous strides; by its close the Battalion had 20 officers and 680 men, doubtless thankful to lay down their arms.

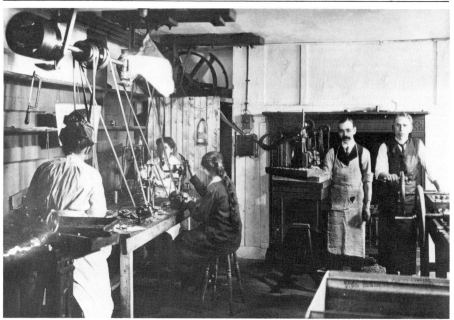

ANOTHER AND LESS REPORTED ACTIVITY took place at 89 Stoke Newington Church Street where a voluntary munitions factory was set up, seen here in operation in 1916.

THE WAR SAW THE FIRST AIR RAIDS ON BRITAIN, and among the missiles dropped was this Zeppelin bomb that fell on Fox Lane, a narrow alley running down from Morning Lane at the back of Trelawny Road, probably in 1916. It was wholesale demolition in the 1950s, not bombing, however, that destroyed the houses in this view.

169 lbs

P.C. EDMUND Forbes

First bomb dropped from
zeppelin on ~~[illegible]~~
Rear of **Nevill Arms** Public
House Stoke Newington

A POLICEMAN'S LOT on this occasion was 169lbs. PC Edmund Forbes is the proud possessor of a bomb that dropped behind the Nevill Arms, Nevill Road on 30 May 1915. Landlady Laura Kirkby had a narrow escape.

THE FIRST LOCAL STREET PARTIES seem to have taken place to celebrate the end of the First World War. This one is well under way in Digby Road in 1919.

STOKE NEWINGTON chose to add a memorial hall to the library with a list of those lost during the war inside. It was opened in June 1923 by Field Marshal Sir William Robertson with due pomp and circumstance.

## SECTION FOUR

# The Changing Scene II

BUSIER STREETS, more traffic, the loss of old buildings and the beginning of large commercial construction – this section looks at each former borough in turn, beginning with Hackney's Mare Street, seen here from the Well Street junction looking north to the railway bridge, with Matthew Rose's store rising above their advert on the bridge.

ASPLANDS WAS A LARGE DRAPERY STORE at 102–8 Kingsland High Street, and is shown here at a grand re-opening in the early 1930s. Asplands did not last long enough to become a household name and had changed hands by 1934.

GROVE HOUSE, 36 Chatham Place was one of the larger houses built at the beginning of the eighteenth century on St Thomas's Hospital estate. It ceased to be a private house in 1890 and after a brief period as a clothing factory, passed to the Hackney Progressive Club in 1900. By the time of this 1912 view it was empty and remained so until demolition in 1921, one of many such buildings to go as the social composition of the area changed.

TWO NOTABLE BUILDINGS on Homerton High Street in 1934 were Ram's Episcopal Chapel, which had closed two years before, and Eagle House, which had been in business use since the 1880s but was then turned into a lodging house. Ram's conservative congregation, one of whom had been so outraged by a change in service that she had threatened the minister with her solicitor, had dwindled away, and the chapel itself was demolished shortly after 1935, while Eagle House survived until the early 1950s.

THE NORTH SIDE OF LEA BRIDGE ROAD at the Clapton end in 1909. The Clapton Cigarette Manufactory and the small shops were all cleared for the Lea Bridge Roundabout in 1970.

SHACKLEWELL was one of the old village centres of Hackney. This is part of Prospect Row, on the north side, in the early 1930s. These late eighteenth-century houses, on the site of premises used as a workhouse, were swept away for a housing scheme in 1936.

NO. 1 KINGSLAND HIGH STREET, about 1930, with traffic having grown enough to need a policeman on point duty, but not enough to prevent him standing in the middle of the road. Purpose built as a bank in 1883, the branch was closed by Barclays in 1990.

THE BRITISH ASYLUM for Deaf and Dumb Females at 179 Lower Clapton Road, seen here in 1930. Founded in 1851, the Asylum moved to Eagle House, Homerton in 1856 before acquiring No. 179 in 1864. When this area of Lower Clapton Road was compulsorily purchased for the first Powell House estate in 1930 there were many protests at the loss of this and other fine early eighteenth-century houses in the neighbourhood, but to no avail. The Asylum moved to 26 Clapton Common, where it remained until about 1986.

THE HALLWAY OF NO. 179 showing the interior fanlight. The top face of the clock has a separate hand set for striking. The house was probably built in 1712 for Markham Eeles, a crockery manufacturer, and the two decorative urns on the gateposts were said to echo this, giving the house its local nickname of 'Piss Pot Hall'.

THE BUSTLE OF TRAFFIC at the junction of Hackney Road and Shoreditch High Street in the early 1920s, with cabs waiting in the rank for a fare. Beyond George Dance's church of 1740 is the Clerk's House of 1735. The toilet and the houses south of the Clerk's House were demolished shortly after 1930. Under boundary changes proposed at the time of writing this side of the High Street will be lost to Hackney.

SHOREDITCH HIGH STREET in the mid-1920s, showing bookstalls opposite shops between Bethnal Green Road and Church (later Redchurch) Street. Road widening proposals put into effect from 1926 closed down this street trade.

THE UNCHANGED FACE of Hackney Road – except for the loss of the trams and the horse traffic. A postcard view adjoining Queen Elizabeth Hospital, c. 1925.

ANOTHER VIEW of Shoreditch High Street, a little further north than the one opposite, with stallholders to the left and the imposing façade of Jeremiah Rotherham's clothing factory on the right. Rotherhams were factors for all sorts of goods associated with textiles, and it was one of many such businesses in Shoreditch. In the distance is the London Theatre of Varieties. Messrs Hill were part of the Shoreditch tobacco trade, centred on Worship Street.

CELEBRATIONS AT HAGGERSTON on the opening of the new St Augustines parish hall in Yorkton Street on 2 July 1927. This was early in the incumbency of the ebullient H.A. Wilson, vicar from 1925 to 1954, a prolific local author whose works included the dramatically named *Death over Haggerston*, based on his wartime experiences.

ANOTHER REMINDER of the large German community of the area was the German Mechanic Society, based at 38 Charles Square and seen here in about 1910. To its right is one of the original houses of the square of 1685. No. 38 was in industrial use by the late 1930s and now stands on the site.

IN THE COURSE OF CHANGE were the Old King John's Head on the corner of Whiston Road and Weymouth Terrace, seen here in 1955 before the area (except for the pub) was cleared for flats. The lower view shows Lipton's bacon warehouse under construction in 1933 on the site of buildings seen at the bottom of p. 42. This was one of the large commercial developments that saw the end of Shoreditch High Street as a shopping area.

THE PRESENT A10 follows the line of the Roman Ermine Street, and was improved as the Stamford Hill Turnpike Road after 1713. The two views on this page and the lower one opposite are from different sections. The top view shows Kingsland High Street looking north from Ridley Road about 1939 and the lower Stoke Newington Road looking north from Palatine Avenue. On the left the domed building is the Apollo Cinema, now the Rio, Hackney's last cinema; beyond it is the spire of Devonshire Square Chapel, which was removed after war damage. A view of around 1925.

ANIMALS ABOUNDING in Stoke Newington Church Street, near the Yoakley Road junction in 1922. Cattle were still being slaughtered in Hackney in the 1920s and some notable escapes from butchers were recorded.

STOKE NEWINGTON HIGH STREET, looking north from the junction with Tyssen Street, about 1925.

THE FORMER PARISH LOCK UP, later No. 8 Lordship Lane, stood on a narrow piece of land behind the Red Lion public house. Built in 1824 in front of the parish pound it was a private house by the time of this 1923 view and has recently been refurbished.

THE LEAFY AVENUES of Woodberry Road near Nos 46–50, looking east to Bethune Road, about 1935. This prosperous area was compulsorily purchased by the LCC for the Woodberry Down Estate in the late 1930s and surviving houses now stand in the renamed Newnton Close.

NORTHUMBERLAND HOUSE, Green Lanes, seen through the lion gateway in 1952. Dating from about 1824, the house was a private lunatic asylum from about 1830 until shortly before its demolition in 1958. Rowley Gardens now occupy the site.

THE BACK OF CHURCH ROW, Stoke Newington Church Street. Built by Job Edwards about 1710 on the site of the old manor house, this splendid terrace was demolished in 1933, shortly after this view was taken, to build the present municipal offices.

STAMFORD HILL was unexceptional in the growth of businesses offering personal services. This 1933 view of Nos 143–9 Stamford Hill shows the premises of Chamberlain and Willows, auctioneers and estate agents, Mrs M. Marriott, hairdresser, the Stamford Hill Café, run by Henry Selley, Grant and Co., House Agents, and stationery retailer, Mrs Margaret Willis.

LIGHT A FIRE, put your feet up and enjoy a good read. This photograph taken in 1935 shows the premises and pavement display of Dear and Sons, coal merchants and corn dealers of 78 Upper Clapton Road. For twopence weekly the Clapton resident could subscribe to the Billet Library next door, run by Miss R. Pinto.

# Shops and Markets

MATTHEW ROSE AND SONS was for many decades the major retailer in Mare Street. Opened in 1867 the business met the drapery and millinery needs of thousands of Hackney ladies and no doubt was a source of the colourful and fine dresses displayed by the young women of Hackney who at the turn of the century could be seen promenading up and down Mare Street every weekend attracting young men in what came to be known as 'Monkey Parades'. This view taken around 1900 shows a parked carriage outside the store behind a horse-drawn tram on its way to Clapton.

HACKNEY'S GEORGE BUSH was a successful hairdresser based at 113 Downs Road. Shown here with his assistant in 1905, the window display suggests that hairdressing extended to shaving, wig and hairpiece fitting and the sale of fancy-dress masks.

THIS INVITING GROCER'S STORE was owned by James Adams and family. They are shown here outside the premises at 7 Morning Lane in 1914.

NEWSAGENT JAMES EDWARD MUNNS of 6 Gainsborough Road in Hackney Wick provided his customers with more tobacco and newspapers before 1914 than was probably good for them. A speciality was the twelve-page *Big Comic*, 'the biggest and best ever published' at one halfpence. To quench the thirst, 'Monsters' lemonade cost one penny.

IF LEMONADE DID NOT SATISFY, Henry George Bradford of 213 Lower Clapton Road provided most alcoholic requirements. The premises appear to have served a dual purpose. The 1898 street directory shows G.P. Bradford acting as deputy registrar of births and deaths for North Hackney and deputy registrar of marriages for the whole of Hackney. It can be presumed that after registering a birth upstairs, the proud parents could then find everything they needed downstairs to wet the baby's head.

RIDLEY ROAD MARKET has maintained its reputation through this century as one of the famous London street markets. A familiar figure was A.E. Craft, fish stall-holder, seen here in the 1930s.

HACKNEY HAS LONG ATTRACTED waves of immigrants, often escaping persecution from their country of origin. Many founded successful businesses to meet the growing demand for goods and services. One such business was the bakers, B. Smulevitch, based at 76 Well Street. This 1930s photograph shows the family, the employees and the guard dog.

THE PICTURESQUE OPEN BUTCHER'S SHOP of E.W. Cincer, trading as the Aberdeen House, was situated on Clapton High Road (later to become Upper Clapton Road) near the junction with Mount Pleasant Lane. The shop remained a retail butchers into the first decade of this century.

ONE OF LONDON'S FIRST further education colleges was the Clark's Business College situated at 147–9 Stamford Hill, shown here in 1912. In the foreground are the staff of Samuel's fruit stall displaying their produce.

STILL A FAMOUS DALSTON LANDMARK is the business of F. Cooke's Eel and Pie Shop. The family business goes back to 1862 when Robert Cooke opened his first shop in Brick Lane. The premises at 41 Kingsland High Street opened in 1910 and was renowned for the beautiful interior tiles, marble, mirrors and stained glass. These two photographs taken in 1955 show the cafe interior and the storage tanks in the back of the shop where the live eels were kept in steel drawers through which water flowed.

MR J.H. HOUSEMAN JP, Shoreditch politician and managing director of Bewells Ltd, pharmaceutical manufacturer and cash chemists, at the counter of his shop at 19–21 Pitfield Street in 1932. One of his products, the 'Little Black Divils', was said to have a wonderful reputation for curing coughs and colds and was excellent for throat and voice. Mr Houseman, a life-long Liberal, was elected as Mayor of Shoreditch in October 1932 and was regarded as mainly responsible for the installation of the wireless at the Pitfield Street Public Library.

THE SHOP FRONTAGE OF ZIBA DUDLEY, Drapers and Milliners of 119–27 Kingsland High Street, is shown here in 1910. Celebrated for its lace curtains, the shop was known as 'The House of Cheapness'. Mr Dudley is just discernible, standing between the rolls of curtain fabric displayed on the pavement.

THE LION FUR STORES of 12 High Street, Stoke Newington was the area's main purveyor of fur fashion accessories in 1909. The shop interior resembled a museum of taxidermy with full-size bears and other growling beasts, and sold 'marvellous cheap stone marten and sable cravats, collaretts, muffs etc. Long ostrich feather boas and ruffles, all colours.'

JAMES BROOKE AND SONS LTD, Home Furnishers of 2 Clarence Road, celebrating in style the 1937 Coronation of King George VI.

THIS LOCAL LANDMARK was situated above the premises of Edward Maund, Shopfitters of 336 Old Street. The photograph is thought to have been taken in 1910.

AMID THE EARLY TWENTIETH-CENTURY EXPANSION of goods and services, Hackney experienced large areas of working-class poverty. This 1899 photograph shows the premises of Brigham Edwin, Pawnbroker of 7–9 Gainsborough Road, Hackney Wick displaying pawned carpets, trousers and even boots.

THE ORIGINAL BUTTERS FAMILY building business was found in the 1840s, but later members of the family also went into the same line. These are George Butters's employees outside the back entrance to his yard at 26 Warnford Street, about 1900, handcarts at the ready.

THOMAS BRYANT UNDERWOOD'S HANDIWORK decorates his own business on 389 Kingsland Road some time after 1905 when he moved there from De Beauvoir Road. A coat of arms over the door gave rise to a spurious story about royal visits: more prosaically it was put up by the previous tenant, another signwriter.

# Business and Industry

Telegraphic Address:
"RENDEVOLE,
LONDON."

Telephone No.
294
DALSTON.

ESTIMATES FREE.

## THOMAS HARRY & Co.

### UPPER CLAPTON DEPOSITORY.

**Furniture Removed and Warehoused** by Road, Rail or Sea.

Chief Office: 109, RENDLESHAM ROAD, HACKNEY DOWNS, N.E.

Branch Office: HIGH ROAD, UPPER CLAPTON    FIREPROOF FURNITURE WAREHOUSE
18a & 18b, Manor Road, Stoke Newington, N.

THERE WERE FEW LARGE FACTORIES in the Hackney area. Shoreditch had the greatest concentration of businesses, principally furniture, shoe and clothing works, with factors for various goods from the 1920s. Hackney's clothing and shoe factories were part of an industrial scene which included confectionary, plastics, paint and chemicals. Stoke Newington had a variety of light industries mostly in former residential premises. Small businesses were characteristic of the whole area and Thomas Harry and Co. was an example of this. Harry started as a greengrocer in Rendlesham Road in 1886, then five years later became a coal merchant and jobmaster, the latter activity forming the basis of the removal business. Harry and Co. even branched out as estate agents in the 1920s, but the removals became the sole business from 1938 until the firm closed in 1975.

THE RESEARCH LABORATORY of Lewis Berger and Co. at their Homerton works about 1909. After poor performance at the end of the nineteenth century, the firm was rescued from the last family managing director and was effectively taken over by an American company in 1906. Reinvestment in the ensuing years considerably improved the position.

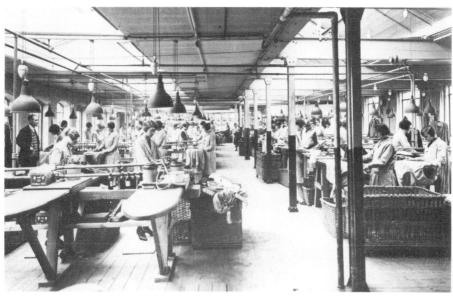

THE SPOTTING DEPARTMENT of dry cleaners Achille Serre, Carpenters Road, in 1927. The founder of this business fifty years before was one of the first to introduce the process to Britain. The firm later moved from industrial Hackney Wick to Walthamstow and was later taken over by Sketchleys.

THE SHOE TRADE spread from Shoreditch to Well Street, South Hackney, by 1890. This interior is part of a typical small factory, location as yet unidentified, in the 1920s.

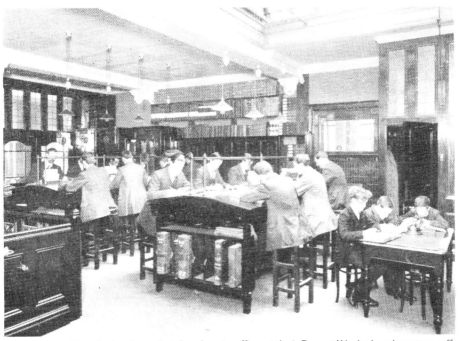

DOTTERIDGES, the wholesale undertakers' main office at their Dorset Works headquarters, off East Road in the early 1920s. The all-male clerks are filling out ledgers and dealing with correspondence, while the juniors sit at scaled-down versions of the high office stools. These working conditions would have been typical of many concerns at this period.

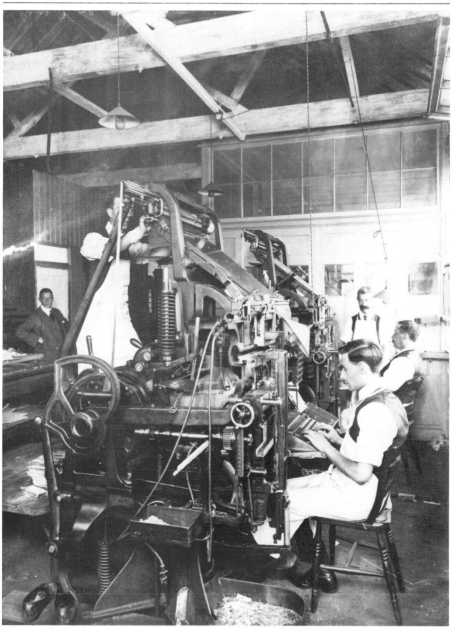

THE *HACKNEY GAZETTE* was founded in 1864 and has had three successive premises, all on the Kingsland Road. Until 1987 the *Gazette* was printed in Hackney and this view of the print room at Nos 440–2 shows the linotype compositing and rotary printing presses in use about 1925.

ALL READY TO GET THE NEWS of Queen Mary's visit to Shoreditch out is this gleaming new *Hackney Gazette* van, outside 442 Kingsland Road, in March 1922.

BENJAMIN POLLOCK in his toy theatre shop, 73 Hoxton Street in 1929. The business had been founded here in 1851. Benjamin died in 1937 but the business carried on in Hoxton until bombed out. The remaining stock and plates were bought out by Mrs Marguerite Fawdry who established the present Pollocks Toy Theatre Museum, still selling the scenes and characters that were once 'penny plain, tuppence coloured'.

CLAPTON BATHS was the scene of a trades fair organized by the Hackney and Stoke Newington Chamber of Commerce to promote employment in the area. The fair was opened by Prince George (later George VI) in November 1933, with help from the mayoral party, including Herbert Ormond. Among the fifty stands were purveyors of furniture, rugs, radios and sausage-making machines. Visitors were entertained by mannequin parades and the strains of Phil Maurice and his Gypsy Orchestra.

Opposite:
SHOREDITCH HAD ITS OWN FILM STUDIOS from 1924–49, housed in a former power station in Poole Street. Founded by American Paramount, the studio was later used by British companies, one of which used the Gainsborough Lady logo for its productions. Films made there included early works of Alfred Hitchcock, with Margaret Lockwood starring in *The Lady Vanishes* and other productions. The still is from *Chu Chin Chow* of 1934, starring George Robey. Financial pressure brought about the closure of the studios in 1949: at the time of writing the building is threatened with demolition.

PLANT NURSERIES had a long history in the area, with the earliest businesses being established in Hoxton in the 1670s. By the end of the last century those that remained were mainly in the northern end of Hackney, catering mostly for local trade as the effects of building and London smoke had forced the larger businesses to move away or close down. Pink's Nursery on Spring Hill was typical of the survivors, adjoining John Such's refreshment room in the Thatched Cottage and shown on this postcard view of the early 1920s.

# More Light, More Power: Local Government

THE EFFECTS OF URBAN GROWTH in the second half of the nineteenth century stimulated the passing of many acts of parliament which conferred duties upon local authorities. Until the creation of the Metropolitan Boroughs in 1900, inner London local services had, with the exception of the London County Council founded in 1889, been in the hands of the small scale committees presided over by the Vestries. This photograph shows the Public Gardens and Open Spaces Committee of the Hackney Vestry shortly before its abolition. Back row: ? Osborne (gardener), C.O. Barber, W.J. Sandwell, E. Holworth, A.A. Everard, ? Cooper and J. Rainbow (superintendent gardener). Middle row: F. Harrison, D.H. Evans, G. Chambers, J.B. Kyfrin, G.Y. Baldock, -?-, W.P.S. Whicher. Front row: -?-, R. Taylor, E.P. Warner, H. Roach (clerk in the Surveyor's Department).

THIS BEAUTIFULLY PROPORTIONED BUILDING was Hackney's second town hall. It was opened in 1866 to accommodate the growing local government service needed for the expanding population of Hackney. This photograph was taken in 1895 before the addition of new wings and shows the extensive public gardens behind the Town Hall across to Hackney Grove.

BY THE 1930S THE TOWN HALL was felt to be inadequate to meet the Borough's needs and replacement was felt to be the only solution. The Town Hall is shown here in 1937 in the process of demolition. The present Town Hall can be seen in the background in the process of construction.

THE PROCLAMATION OF THE ACCESSION of King Edward VII being read on the steps of Hackney Town Hall by the Mayor, Viscount Horncastle, in January 1901.

THE PHOTOGRAPHIC RECORDS of the early years of the Stoke Newington Metropolitan Borough include many portraits and images of the mayors attending dinners and foundations, often dressed in their heavy fur-trimmed robes. These great self-publicists came together for yet another dinner on 9 February 1914 where they posed for a group photograph. Back row: Cllr W. Thatcher 1912–13, Cllr T.H. Gee-Moore 1911–12, Cllr H.J. Beavis 1910–11, Alderman J.R. Brough 1910–11. Middle row: Sidney White (Town Clerk), Cllr J.L. Sheffield 1908–9, Alderman W.S. Wright 1907–8, Alderman W.B. Trick JP 1906–7, Alderman W.S. Savery JP 1905–6, Alderman E.C. Price 1904–5. Front row: Alderman A. Johnston 1902–3, Cllr Sir John Runtz JP 1900–1, The Rt. Hon. Lord Mayor of London, Alderman H.J. Ormond 1913–14, Alderman W. Eve 1901–2, Cllr J.G. Glass JP 1903–4.

THE LORD MAYOR OF LONDON, Sir George Broadbridge receiving councillors at the opening of the new Stoke Newington Town Hall on 28 September 1937. Note the uncanny resemblance of his daughter to a former Prime Minister.

SEEN HERE TAKING HIS CIVIC DUTIES to new heights is Cllr J.S. Baker, Mayor of Shoreditch, visiting the Hoxton Sun Babies Hostel in October 1934 as part of the Borough's Health and Baby Week programme. Did the mace bearer find this outing as enjoyable as the Mayor seems to have done?

THE SPLENDID CONCERT HALL and ballroom in Shoreditch Town Hall, the scene of many entertainments, supported by the Borough. This photograph appeared in the 1940 edition of the *Shoreditch Borough Guide*, an annual publication, which described the extensive range of activities undertaken by the Metropolitan Borough.

SEWER REPLACEMENT by Hackney Metropolitan Borough in Albion Square in 1951.

THE HACKNEY METROPOLITAN BOROUGH ELECTRICITY GENERATING STATION at Millfields viewed here across the River Lea Navigation Cut in 1937.

BEFORE THE SECOND WORLD WAR local authorities had greater powers than they do in the late twentieth century. Shoreditch claimed to be the first district in England to utilize the heat generated by burning its refuse for electricity, hence the motto on the Borough Arms – 'More Light, More Power'. The top photograph shows an Electricity Supply Department Exhibition held in 1904 at the Pitfield Street Baths. Below is the Borough Electricity Showroom in Old Street, floodlit to celebrate the 1935 Silver Jubilee.

THE NEWLY FORMED METROPOLITAN BOROUGHS sought to provide indoor swimming baths for safety and recreational purposes. Shown here is the Kings Hall Baths in Lower Clapton Road shortly after its opening at the turn of the century.

THE STOKE NEWINGTON LIBRARY SERVICES provided a range of activities beyond the loan of books. In 1939 a local history exhibition took place reflecting the public interest in the rich history of the area.

THE HACKNEY METROPOLITAN BOROUGH Library Services' contribution to the Coronation festivities in 1953. Shown here is the 'Queen' of the Children's Library service, atop her float, presumably enjoying the latest edition of *Biggles*.

THE PITFIELD STREET PUBLIC LIBRARY was opened in April 1898 and in common with other libraries in those days, housed its chief librarian. The library shown here c. 1920, was the gift of Mr J. Passmore Edwards who was also the benefactor of Shoreditch's other library, the Haggerston Library on Kingsland Road, a fine building which is now sadly derelict.

A HACKNEY ROAD SAFETY EXHIBITION for school children, c. 1955.

THE HACKNEY 'GRIME SQUAD' pictured in front of the Town Hall with their latest equipment in 1948.

# Public Health and Housing

BEFORE THE NATIONAL HEALTH SERVICE, local authorities were required under Acts of Parliament to promote activities to improve the health of the nation. Hackney was at the forefront of disease prevention in the 1930s and provided services which encompassed sanitation, overcrowding and slum clearance, improvement in diet, diptheria prevention and the eradication of household pests. Publicity campaigns were mounted to educate the public, with many activities aimed at schoolchildren, some using exhibitions and films. The Borough made at least two films – *Slum Clearance and Re-Housing in the Borough* and *Food Supply and Food Inspection in the Borough* – as well as buying in such films as *A Brush With the Enemy* produced by the Dental Board of the United Kingdom and *Dirty Bertie* produced by the Health and Cleanliness Council. The films formed part of travelling exhibitions around the Borough. The photograph shows the residents of Gainsborough Square, Hackney Wick who turned out to see an exhibition on personal cleanliness in May 1935.

AN OFFICER from the Public Health Department purchasing milk samples from a Hackney grocer's shop, c. 1953. Analysis of food was carried out not only to ensure a safe food supply but also to check for food adulteration such as additives and colouring.

FOOD INSPECTION at an unidentified fishmonger's stall, c. 1953.

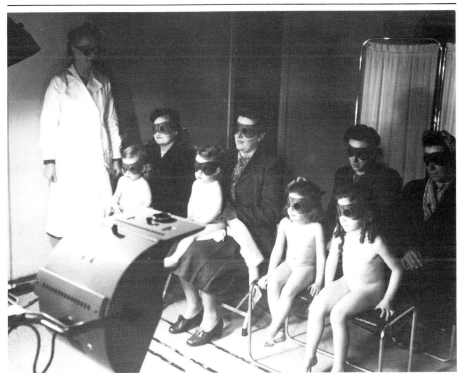

CHILDREN UNDERGOING ARTIFICIAL SUNLIGHT TREATMENT at the Maternity and Child Welfare Clinic in Richmond Road, c. 1949. Artificial sunlight was used to treat rickets, anaemia, debility and, above all, malnutrition with 122 cases being treated at this clinic in 1937. It was also given to expectant and nursing mothers to relieve strain and general infirmity.

THE LAUNDRY ROOM at the Disinfecting Station, Millfields Road in 1935. Articles were removed from houses following infectious disease and either disinfected or destroyed. Some 42,562 items of clothing and bedding were either destroyed or treated in 1937 alone.

THE STEAM DISINFECTION of household goods in a sealed pantechnicon at the Millfields Cleansing Station in 1937.

INFESTATION OF HOUSES by bed bugs was usually caused by the transfer of belongings from house to house. Methods of eradication varied according to conditions. In some cases the premises were fumigated by sealing rooms and burning sulphur dioxide. A charge of two shillings and sixpence a room was made for this treatment except in cases of extreme poverty. Early or slight infection was dealt with, as in the photograph, using sprays which were sometimes sold to tenants.

THE INTERIOR of a slum prior to spraying, C. 1934.

COMBINED LIVING AND SLEEPING ROOM in an unknown slum premises, C. 1934.

HACKNEY EMBARKED UPON a radical five-year slum clearance programme from 1930 to 1935, informed by reports from the Medical Officer of Health. Cases for demolition were referred to public enquiries where the Property Owners' Protection Association, representing the landlords, vigorously opposed demolition. A small selection of the properties earmarked for demolition are shown on this and the following pages. The top photograph shows the gardens and backs of houses in College Street and Homerton Row off Homerton High Street. Note the outside toilets. The area was replaced by Banister House, opened in July 1935, which provided accommodation for 768 persons.

OTLEY TERRACE, off Lea Bridge Road, providing a windowless world to the luckless inhabitants. An allegation was made at the 1933 public enquiry that Hackney Council were seeking to pull down the houses so that they could buy the land cheaply, but the enquiry found in favour of the Council.

CONDUIT COURT, shown here in 1929, in the Northwold Road clearance area, which, despite the poor housing conditions, housed a small, lively community. Note the tin bath on the wall.

HEYWOOD BUILDINGS in the Banister Street clearance area off Homerton High Street providing a safe play area, if not a sanitary home. The area was replaced by Banister House in July 1935.

NOT ALL SLUM CLEARANCE was confined to urban areas. The relatively rural Spring Lane did not escape the fight against slum conditions, these houses being subject to compulsory purchase orders placed before the Council in March 1937.

A PUBLIC ENQUIRY was held in April 1937 into the alleged unfitness for public habitation of Nos 2–5 Swiss Cottages situated at the corner of Wetherell Road and Lauriston Road, overlooking the Jews' Burial Ground.

THE DEMOLITION of part of the Broadway Market area formed part of the five-year programme. Shown here are Nos 5–7 Duncan Road, abutting onto Duncan Square. These streets were replaced by Duncan House.

NOS 6–10 CHURCHYARD, which faced north towards the Old Church Tower overlooking Hackney Churchyard. These houses were subject to a clearance order placed before the Council in May 1937 and had probably been demolished prior to the area being devastated by a bomb on the night of 19–20 March 1941.

A HACKNEY RESIDENT hanging out the washing at 45 Shacklewell Lane in the 1930s. The house shows severe signs of settlement to the arches and windows and throughout the lines of the brickwork.

THIS VIEW IS TYPICAL of the courtyard developments that existed in the area of Shoreditch which abutted onto the City of London and shows W.H. Brooks, chimney sweeper and carpet beater outside his premises at 5 Queens Square, off Finsbury Avenue. The area stood on the site of the Broadgate development.

THESE ATTRACTIVE SINGLE-STOREY COTTAGES, known as Caroline Cottages, were situated half-way down Caroline Street, off Rossington Street, Upper Clapton. The area was demolished in 1935 as part of a London County Council clearance scheme to make way for Ettrick and Charnwood Houses which were opened in September 1937.

MR HENRY JAMES PLUMLEY and companion outside No. 10 Barn Street, off Stoke Newington Church Street, prior to demolition to make way for the Denman House development opened in 1934.

THESE TWO VIEWS from the turn of the century show Mr and Mrs James Brown at home at 2 Handley Road, South Hackney. They are included in the selection because the modest terraced property had a curious summer house in the back garden. Mr Brown was councillor for Homerton Ward from 1912–16.

THE MIDDLE-CLASS LAYMAN FAMILY posing in their living room at 199 Green Lanes in the 1920s.

VALETTE BUILDINGS, Valette Street was one of the earliest examples of publicly owned housing in Hackney. Built by the London County Council in 1904 on the site of the former Jerusalem Square and Passage, it housed skilled working-class tenants and was built partly in response to an appeal by the Trades' Council to relieve the high unemployment of building workers in the East End.

THE OFFICIAL OPENING of Lordship House, Stoke Newington in 1934 by the Minister of Health, Hilton Young, accompanied by Mayor Alderman Gordon.

THE STOKE NEWINGTON HOUSING COMMITTEE inspecting building progress at Amwell Court in 1948.

KING GEORGE VI AND QUEEN ELIZABETH inspecting the flat of Mr and Mrs C. Whitaker at Hillcot House on the newly built Stonebridge Estate, Haggerston in March 1938. The Queen was said to have been especially impressed by the spacious balconies and the electric fires, the King with the low rents. Hillcot House was the last block to be demolished on the estate in 1991.

NISBET HOUSE, Homerton photographed in 1938 shortly after opening. The estate replaced Nisbet Street, Fulham Place, Clarence Terrace, Austin's Buildings and Pear Tree Court which had clearance orders placed on them by the Minister of Health in 1934.

THIS LIVELY PHOTOGRAPH shows Aneurin Bevan, the Minister of Health, being accosted by an irate tenant at the opening of Fairchild House on the Pitfield Estate, Shoreditch in September 1950.

THE OFFICIAL OPENING of the Forest Road Estate, Dalston by Mayor Councillor G.C. Carter in October 1948.

HACKNEY'S FIRST ESTATE, Powell House, is shown here in a commemorative aerial photograph in 1934. It stood on the site of the former British Deaf and Dumb Asylum and other early eighteenth-century houses and provided 198 flats for 900 persons. Beyond economic repair by the late 1970s Powell House was demolished in the early 1980s.

THE MORNINGSIDE ESTATE CLUBROOM with tenants and children in August 1954.

A TYPICAL LIVING ROOM at Edred House on the Kingsmead Estate, c. 1950.

NOT ALL HOUSING WAS DEMOLISHED on public health grounds. Here are two examples of attractive and solidly built housing, demolished simply because they were deemed unfashionable. The top photograph shows the former terrace of houses at 371–413 Kingsland Road which backed onto Lockner Road, forming the east side of De Beauvoir Square. The photograph was taken during the Second World War and shows how close the houses came to taking a direct bomb hit. The houses were pulled down in the late 1960s.

NICHOLS SQUARE, off the Hackney Road, shortly before demolition by Shoreditch Borough Council in 1963. The decision to demolish the fine 1840s square was loudly condemned in the architectural press but the Council decision prevailed, destroying the long-standing local community and creating in its stead the Fellows Court development.

# Poverty and Sickness

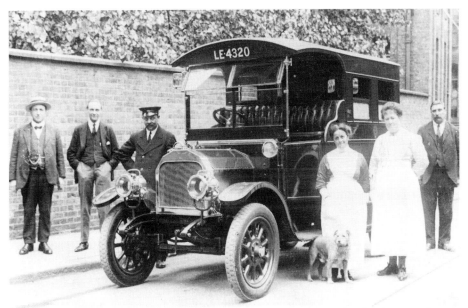

AS WELL AS MAKING PROVISION for its own poor, Hackney was home to the almshouses of many other bodies and institutions. Hospital provision grew out of services provided by work-houses, supplemented by voluntary clinics. The twentieth century saw the closure of many of the Shoreditch almshouses as the area became more industrial and the emergence of hospitals as separate bodies after the abolition of workhouses in 1930. This opening view shows the Hackney Workhouse Infirmary motor ambulance, with staff and Matron's dog, about 1919.

WHEELCHAIR PROVISION was a thing of the future: a Hackney pauper in motion, either at the Homerton site or the Brentwood annexe, c. 1900.

EACH OF THE HACKNEY WORKHOUSE BUILDINGS was identified by a letter. This is the interior of 'H' block, showing the women's ward. The bare boards, uniforms, caps and aprons speak of the grim helplessness the 'bun house' created amongst working people.

THE NORTH SIDE OF 'F' BLOCK. The Union workhouse, dating from 1837, served Hackney and Stoke Newington. As Hackney Hospital it remains in use for geriatric patients in 1991.

IT WAS A PRINCIPLE that paupers should work, but not in tasks that might compete with local industry. This was one of the answers: the stone breaking yard at Gainsborough Road (now Eastway), again about 1900.

WELFARE OF A MORE HUMANE KIND was provided by the Salvation Army, who took over Maitland Place, Lower Clapton Road (dating from 1824) as a maternity hospital. Initially for unmarried mothers, it proved so popular that many of Hackney's children were born here until it closed in 1986.

HACKNEY WAS EARLY in the hospice movement. This is the entrance to St Josephs Hospice, founded in 1905 by the Irish Sisters of Charity. The house on the right is the last of Cambridge Lodge Villas, incorporated into the hospice and demolished in 1965. No. 1 had been General William Booth's home in the 1860s – he is said to have been driven away by the bells of the nearby Cambridge Heath Congregational Church. This Mare Street view dates from the early 1950s.

HACKNEY'S SUBSTANTIAL GERMAN COMMUNITY in happier times, turning out for the third visit by the Kaiserin to the German Hospital on 18 May 1911, part of a trip made for the coronation of George V.

THE FRONT OF THE GERMAN HOSPITAL and the Lutheran Hamburg Church, seen from across the North London Railway line in 1899. This is the 1865 building, with later extensions.

PAROCHIAL ALMSHOUSES were still flourishing at the turn of the century. These were West Hackney Almshouses. Originally built in Cooks Rents in 1737, the buildings were donated by the Tyssen family, lords of the manor, to West Hackney parish and opened after a subscription in 1842. These were the new buildings of 1889, on the north side of the road and are still used as almshouses today.

THE COURTYARD OF ST SCHOLASTICAS RETREAT, Kenninghall Road. Founded in 1861 by Charlotte Harrison for reduced Catholic gentry, the almshouses were designed by Pugin and opened in 1864. This view was taken around 1900 and the almshouses lasted until the mid-1970s. It is now part of the site of St Scholasticas School.

AN ALMSWOMAN by her door in the north corner of the Bishops Woods Almshouses, Clapton Pond, about 1910. With reputedly the smallest chapel in Britain, the almshouses, founded in 1690, have recently been converted from ten to five dwellings to give the almswomen more space.

ALMSHOUSES WERE ON THE WAIN in Shoreditch when this 1907 view was taken. This was the Frameworkers, Kniters or Bourne's Almshouse, just to the north of the present Geffrye Museum on Kingsland Road. Built in 1734, the City livery company had already moved its almsmen out to Oadby, Leicestershire by 1907 and a factory now covers the site.

NOT ALL ALMSHOUSES moved as far away as Leicestershire. Shoreditch parochial almshouses, formerly on the Hackney Road just north of Waterson Street, were rebuilt at Wood Green in 1904, and the Hackney Road site is now a garden. The top view shows the Wood Green frontage in 1906 while the lower catches a tea party in progress in the back garden a year before.

HOXTON CHRISTIAN MARKET MISSION was founded in 1881 by John and Lewis Burtt, initially as missionary activity undertaken by Rectory Road Congregational Church, Hackney. The top view shows Lewis Burtt, the secretary (wearing bowler and monocle), James Stuart, the local MP and friends on or shortly after the opening of the new institute in July 1892. In the lower view of 1910 Burtt is surrounded by the Mission's brass band, prior to a musical evening.

THE MISSION PROVIDED OUTINGS, holidays, clothes and food to the Hoxton poor, and was known locally as 'Daddy Burtt's'. This page and the top view of the facing one show Christmas food handouts around 1950. Cakes and cornflakes to the fore!

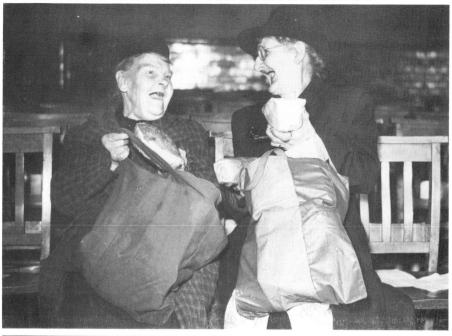

Below:

THE RELIGIOUS SIDE OF THE MISSION is caught here, with Sister Florence reading the lesson to a men's meeting in 1935 – before lunch judging by their expressions. The Mission survived bombing in the Second World War, but social changes in the area gradually diminished its role, while its donations also shrank. The end came in 1983, though the Hoxton Market building still bears a sign proclaiming its origin.

THE NEW AND THE OLD: the R20 airship over Livermere Road, Haggerston, about 1930, and an animated view of horse-drawn vehicles by the North London station of the LMS, Shoreditch High Street, about 1920. The woman cyclist is a sign of changing times, though she may have dismounted to avoid trams sweeping round from Hackney Road behind her.

View from High St. Shoreditch.

# Getting About

CANALS, RIVER, ROAD AND RAIL all played their part in moving people and goods around and through the area. With the rise of motor buses in the 1920s railways faced increased competition, but lorries and trains had not yet wholly supplanted canals. This 1950 view shows the Regents Canal looking east towards the Whitmore Road bridge. The canal was opened in 1820, but in recent years the industry that lined its banks has given way to housing and its role as a bulk carrier has come to an end.

A HORSE-DRAWN TRAM heads south on Lower Clapton Road drawing level with the Deaf & Dumb Asylum entrance, with the large houses facing Clapton Pond and the spire of the Wesleyan Chapel in the background. It was not until 1909 that this route was electrified.

ELECTRIC TRAMS pass by West Hackney Church, Stoke Newington Road, about 1910. Trolleybuses replaced the trams in 1938. West Hackney Church in this form is also no more, as it was destroyed during the Second World War.

A BUSY SCENE LOOKING SOUTH from Nos 21–30 Shoreditch High Street. An 'A' type tram (the last of which went in 1931) has just come in from Chingford Mount. Nicholls & Clarke are still at their High Street address supplying paint and building materials, but the chimney, adjoining the course of the eastern lines out of Liverpool Street Station, has now been demolished.

MANOR HOUSE TRAM INTERCHANGE, after the opening of the new tube station in September 1932. 'C' class tram No. 24 is on the 27 route, running then from Tottenham Court Road to Edmonton.

WHAT A TO-DO on Kingsland Road! One of Sutton's horse vans has just rushed out of Richmond Road and collided with a 76 bus on the afternoon of 16 June 1927. Two women suffering from shock were taken to the nearby Metropolitan Hospital, but no-one else was hurt.

GEORGE EWER'S GREY GREEN COACH STATION, 55 Stamford Hill, and an array of Bedford Duplex coaches, about 1947. Ewer began hiring out coaches in 1885 and the family business acquired its first motors in 1919, moving to Stamford Hill in 1930.

ONE OF WILLIAM ADAMS 4-4-0 TANKS west bound on a Broad Street train at Hackney Station in 1927. This was the last year of the outside cylinder passenger tanks, dating from 1868, and many services were still using the old four-wheeled stock until the early 1930s. The North London Railway had suffered badly from road competition from the early years of the century, and the passenger service between Dalston and Poplar was withdrawn in 1944. Happily this was restored in the 1980s, though the Broad Street city line is no more.

HACKNEY'S ONLY TUBE STATION is Manor House on the Piccadilly Line, opened in 1932, as part of an extension from Finsbury Park to Arnos Grove. This photograph shows the joining of the old and new tunnels near Finsbury Park in 1931.

GREAT EXCURSIONS: the Gibbons family of the 'Cash Only' furniture store on Amhurst Road are about to set off from their Kenmure Road home, about 1900.

NATHAN LEIBOVITCH'S ANNUAL WORKS OUTING ready for the off from near the firm's cabinet-making business in Hoxton Square in the mid-1920s.

# SECTION ELEVEN

# Keeping Amused

THE NEW CENTURY offered more opportunities for recreation. Motor transport ensured that local outings could go further afield without being dependent on the railway and local horse brakes. Theatre and music hall faced a strong challenge from the new cinemas – appearing from 1908 onwards. But older pursuits, self-improvement and social activities of all kinds flourished. This float in Stoke Newington Church Street sometime in the Boer War period is probably engaged in some form of fund raising, though as yet no further evidence has come to light.

TWO CONSTRASTING NUPTIALS: the Arnall family wedding at 393 Kingsland Road, about 1910 (above), and the rather more grand wedding of Doris Butters and David Haler in the back garden of 3 Springfield in 1933. Both houses have now gone – the Arnall house for Blandford House in the late 1960s and No. 3 Springfield in 1937, again for council housing.

MAYORAL JINKS at a fund-raising garden party for the Metropolitan Hospital held in the back gardens of 83–5 Lordship Road. One of the hosts was Mayor Herbert Ormond, seen hurling at a coconut shy with his fellow mayors Cllrs Bloomfield (Hackney) and Bennett (Bethnal Green). The women were modelling bathing suits from Dudleys, the drapers of Kingsland High Street on a chilly June day in 1933 and competing with the rival attraction of a comic dog show. Mayor Ormond would appear to be looking for a thick ear rather than having his fortune told.

GIRLS HARD AT WORK at the Clapton School of Art, shortly before it closed in June 1916. Founded at 37 Clapton Common, the school moved to No. 81 in 1888. The local historian Florence Bagust taught there, and took this photograph, as well as recording the loss of grant from the LCC which brought on the closure.

FANCY DRESS from the Stoke Newington Rotary Club, united as Jugoslavia, about 1935.

THE CLAPTON RINK CINEMA COSTUME CONCERT COMPANY in full voice about 1914. After its brief period as a skating rink, the cinema at 137 Lower Clapton Road remained in business until 1942 and was demolished in the 1950s.

MUSICAL ACCOMPANIMENT of a different kind at the Alexandra Theatre was provided by Stanley Holt's Alexandra Theatre orchestra, seen here with conductor Leonard Leask in the early 1920s. The theatre at 67–9 Stoke Newington Road, opened in 1897 and closed in October 1950.

THE ROYAL CAMBRIDGE MUSIC HALL, 136 Commercial Street, seen shortly after re-opening in 1899. The previous building of 1864 had been burnt down three years before. Closed in 1936, the site is now covered by a factory.

THE BACK SEAT AT THE MOVIES would never be the same again as the Standard Theatre, Goldsmith's Row was rebuilt after these photographs were taken in May 1927. In its new guise the cinema, dating from 1916, carried all before it until *The Creature from the Black Lagoon* quite literally closed the show in 1960.

THE TWENTIETH CENTURY saw the decline of Shoreditch theatre. The top view shows the queue for the gallery outside the Standard Theatre, 203–4 Shoreditch High Street, about 1900. From its origins as a public house first licensed for entertainment in 1837, the Standard's great days were in the 1880s and '90s, when little boys were employed to make artificial waves in a huge tank on stage. After 1926 the Standard was a cinema, closing in 1939. The London Music Hall (below) replaced the Griffin Musical Hall in 1896. Designed by theatre architect Frank Matcham it became the Shoreditch Theatre in 1925 and was demolished in 1934.

THE PAVILION CINEMA, 290 Mare Street, was purpose-built in 1914. It had an active Children's Club and the lower view shows the BBC recording members making poles for banners in the early 1950s. *Carry on at Your Convenience* was the last attraction in 1973 and the site is now a bank and council offices.

ANNUAL OUTING for the male regulars of the Prince Arthur public house, Brunswick Place,

Hoxton. View taken before the off, 1920.

THE CLAPTON ORIENT TEAM of 1925/6, photographed at the Millfields ground. The Club had been founded in 1888 and joined the professional league in 1904. In 1905 the club applied and was elected to the second division of the Football League. The majority of the players volunteered for active service in the First World War and most failed to return. The Club retained its name until 1946 when it became known as Leyton Orient.

CHARLES FISHER YATES, the Mayor of Hackney from 1933–4, is shown here presenting the Middlesex Schools' Trophy to the Hackney Schoolboys football team after their 3–2 defeat of Fulham Boys at the Eton Manor ground in November 1933.

# The Sporting Life

MODEL SAILING AND POWER-BOAT RACING were a popular leisure activity in the 1920s and 1930s. The Hackney and North East London Model Yacht Club, inaugurated in September 1928, is shown here at one of their first meetings at Clapton Common Pond. The now demolished Buccleuch Terrace is shown in the background.

THE OPENING CEREMONY of the expanded and improved Clissold Park Bowling Green in 1909, following a campaign to the Parks Committee of the London County Council to provide adequate competition facilities in the Park. The Clissold Park Club had long been overshadowed by the neighbouring Brownswood Club, one of the top league competitors in England, and sought to achieve comparable facilities to compete fully against Brownswood and other clubs.

THE BROWNSWOOD TENNIS CLUB in Green Lanes overlooking the West Reservoir in around 1935. By 1911 the successful Brownswood Bowling Club had outgrown its ground at Kings Road. New premises were obtained on land adjoining 256 Green Lanes and were a major attraction for three decades providing not only bowls but tennis, croquet, putting, archery and billiards, as well as refreshments. The Club closed by 1940 to make way for the proposed Woodberry Down Estate.

THE CLAPTON PREMIER SKATING RINK (also known as the Palais de Dance) was opened in December 1909 with special skating exhibitions given by Miss Bertha Mack, the world's leading skate dancer – 'The Season's Sensation on Roller Skates. The last word in costumes'. Although the owners of the Rink, the Premier Rink Company, confidently emphasized in their publicity material that 'Rinking is the Rage' the business barely lasted eighteen months before conversion to a cinema.

SHOWN HERE EXHIBITING THEIR CRICKETING PROWESS are members of the Stoke Newington Occupational Centre cricket team in the 1930s. Such centres provided practical skills training for the unemployed and were often run by the church or other voluntary organizations.

THIS TRANQUIL VIEW shows the 1910 junior pairs winners of the Spartan Rowing Club regatta. The Club was based at Radley's Boathouse on the River Lea.

THE RIVER LEA branch of the National Rowing Association photographed with their opponents in 1921 after the annual race on the Calais Canal against the Emulation Nautique de Calais. Records suggest that the French team were usually the victors, but in 1921 the Hackney crew triumphed. Mr W.J. Rawlings, Hackney resident and Honorary Secretary of the Lea Branch of the National Rowing Association, is second from the left in the seated row.

ENGLAND EXPERIENCED A SERIOUS EARTH TREMOR on the night of 7 June 1931 which caused much structural damage. Shown here is the aftermath of a burst water main in Great Eastern Street, Shoreditch, believed to have been caused by the earthquake.

THE BOARD OF GUARDIANS of St John at Hackney sought to provide rudimentary vocational training to the unemployed and destitute. Here the foundation stone is being laid to the annexe of the Hackney Training School building at Brentwood, Essex in 1885.

# 'Read All About It': Politics and Special Events

DESPITE THE PROMISE of 'Homes fit for heroes', post-war Shoreditch experienced chronic poverty and unemployment. In September 1921 over 1,000 unemployed men, having held a rally outside Hoxton Church, marched to the premises of the Guardians of the parish of St Leonards in Kingsland Road demanding either employment or adequate maintenance. The Guardians proposed various relief measures but these were rejected by the delegation. The photograph shows the marching unemployed, supported by many employed sympathizers.

SEEN HERE IN 1951 supporting the re-election to Parliament of David Weitzman, the Labour MP for Stoke Newington and Hackney North, is Councillor Sammy Fisher.

Opposite:
HACKNEY POLITICS has rarely been without controversy. This is Horatio Bottomley, newly elected Liberal MP for South Hackney in 1906. Bottomley had been declared bankrupt in 1891 following the collapse of his publishing activities but turned his hand to finance and in a little over ten years had promoted over fifty companies. Charged with fraud in 1909 and acquitted, he resigned his seat in 1912 but such was his local popularity he was re-elected as an Independent in 1918. In May 1922 he was found guilty of fraud and sentenced to seven years' imprisonment. He died in 1933.

Right:
THE LIBERAL ASSOCIATION HEADQUARTERS at Cremer House, Shoreditch in 1929 supporting the election of Harold Reckitt to Parliament.

THE 1910 HAGGERSTON POSTER WAR, when rival flyposter supporters habitually covered the opposing party's advertisements, often leading to unpleasant exchanges. This election was unexpectedly won by H.G. Chancellor, the Liberal candidate, an advocate of temperance reform who overturned the Conservative majority in what the *Daily Graphic* described as 'One of the Greatest Triumphs of East London'.

MEMBERS OF THE HACKNEY INDEPENDENT LABOUR PARTY, including Albert Cullington, on a Sunday outing to Epping in 1923. The Clarion Movement was active in the early socialist struggle but its newspaper and pacifist ideology fell from favour during the First World War.

THE UNSAVOURY SIDE of Hackney politics. The windows of Jewish-owned shops were smashed following a meeting of the British Union of Fascists in Victoria Park in 1936.

QUEEN MARY looking less than amused with Councillor Herbert Ormond on her visit to Stoke Newington in December 1933 to open the Occupational and Recreational Centre.

HUNDREDS OF SHOREDITCH RESIDENTS welcome Queen Mary to Ware Street in March 1922. The Queen, said to be concerned about the living conditions of the poor, paid a surprise visit to the home of Mr and Mrs Joseph Gosling at No. 13, where she found the two adults and their seven children living in the small terraced house with damp walls and crumbling plaster.

THIS DRAMATIC PHOTOGRAPH shows the fire at St John at Hackney on 18 May 1955. After the fire the north and south pediments on the church were removed and changes made to the interior.

BRAINS TRUST, a BBC radio and television favourite of the 1940s and '50s paying a visit to Hackney's Central Hall, c. 1948. The panel included chairman and comedian Kenneth Horne, regular participant Humphrey Lestocq and borough officials including G.L.A. Downing, the Town Clerk. Half the panel appear to be wearing overcoats – was Central Hall suffering a heating problem that night?

# 'Take cover': Second World War

HACKNEY'S PROXIMITY to the City of London and the docks ensured that it was bombed heavily in the Blitz. The worst local incident was in Coronation Avenue, Stoke Newington, when a five-storey block of flats was hit on the night of 13 October 1940 and collapsed, burying 160 people. Of the three boroughs only Hackney kept an extensive photographic record of incidents and this has been drawn on to give an indication of damage and Air Raid Precautions activity. In Haggerston, the local vicar, H.A. Wilson, was caught eating junket by the first air raid sirens and the smells of that and a nearby geranium always came to his mind thereafter. This page shows the aftermath of bombing in 1941, with people on their way to work.

THE HIGHLIGHT of Wings for Victory Week in March 1943 at Clapton Baths was the sinking of a model battleship standing in for the *Bismarck* to the accompanying noise of dive bombers and guns. 'The vessel was sunk by torpedo [in the deep end of the baths] amid joyous acclamation ... ' The real *Bismarck* had been sunk in May 1941.

THE 'CAPTAIN' of the mock-up submarine model HMS *Thrasher* poses with his ship in a Shoreditch council yard at the start of Warship Week, 21 March 1942. The real submarine was adopted by Shoreditch and the model was used in fund-raising efforts.

WITH THE ONSET OF THE WAR in September 1939, there was a mass evacuation of mothers and children from London, followed by a later evacuation of schools. It is likely that this view shows Hackney evacuees on March station, about to set out for country destinations.

ON THE HOME FRONT salvage drivers were important in raising funds. Here is Hackney's mayor, Albert Cullington, opening a book drive outside the Town Hall in June 1943.

STOKE NEWINGTON did its bit in the Second World War as well as the first. This page shows one of the stands at Stoke Newington Town Hall in the War Weapons exhibition on 17–24 May 1941 and a march past by service personnel in the same week.

THE NIGHT OF 8 SEPTEMBER 1940 saw a heavy raid on Hackney. Damage included 42 Cressett Street (above) and 9 St Thomas Square. It was to be post-war clearance rather than bombing that destroyed St Thomas Square.

HOUSE IN MENTMORE TERRACE after a raid on the following night, 9 September 1940.

THE BRITANNIA PUBLIC HOUSE in Mare Street lost its top floor during a raid on 23/24 September 1940. Repaired after the Blitz, it was rebuilt in 1957–8.

THE EAST SIDE OF CHURCH CRESCENT in South Hackney was badly damaged by bombing on 10/11 October 1940. Overhead repairs are in progress to trolley-bus wires shortly afterwards.

ONE OF HACKNEY'S MORE SERIOUS LOSSES was Brooke House, dating from the late fifteenth century. Initial damage caused the evacuation of its mentally ill occupants, but extensive damage by a V1 in 1944 ruined it beyond what was then regarded as repairable. The remains were cleared away in 1954–5. Panelling at Harrow School and a wall painting at the Museum of London are all that survives.

LINSCOTT ROAD was damaged on 15/16 October 1940. The Salvation Army headquarters, Congress Hall, escaped. After the Army moved out in 1970, most of the hall, which began life as the London Orphan Asylum in 1825, was demolished and only the central portico and flanking pillars survive.

SOME OF HACKNEY'S house clearance was the work of the Luftwaffe. This view was taken from the site of 238 Frampton Park Road after a raid on 16 October 1940.

THE RAID of 19/20 March 1941 in the second intensive period of the Blitz hit the centre of Hackney badly. The Railway Tavern, above, was completely rebuilt after the war, as were the shops south of the Old Church Tower. Beyond lies the site of Chalgrove Road, later occupied by pre-fabs and now a car park.

HACKNEY LOST A NUMBER of its churches in the war. The top view shows the front of Mare Street Baptist Church, damaged once in 1940 and hit again in 1945 and demolished after the war. The site is now 143 Mare Street. Below is the cleared shell of St Faith's Church, Londesborough Road in 1946. The parish was later combined with St Matthias, Wordsworth Grove.

LOCAL AUTHORITIES were responsible for air raid precautions wardens and rescue staff. This group (above) was taken outside the yellow subterranean shelter on Lebons Corner, Dalston Lane in 1940. Between the raids rescue squads were on alert, and rather than do nothing, they put their hands to a variety of good works. The lower view shows the Millfields Light Rescue 'A' shift making toys for Hackney Day Nurseries in 1942.

RESCUE WORKERS taking a tea-break at a mobile canteen in Wick Road provided by Eton Manor Cadets, about 1941. Eton Manor Club for Boys had grown out of missionary work at the Wick by old Etonians and was founded in 1909. It was closed during the war.

FOOD FOR BOMB VICTIMS. One of Stoke Newington's food stalls is being provisioned by a van from the Food Flying Squad, which had been bought with funds raised from what is now Tanzania. This 1940 view was taken during a visit to Stoke Newington by Eleanor Roosevelt, wife of the US President.

PLENTY MORE WHERE THAT CAME FROM! Fookes' bakers shop, 370 Wick Road in 1942.

RELIEF SUPPLIES OF FOOD were distributed through a variety of channels, including libraries: this is Stoke Newington reference library in action as a food office later in the war.

FOOD OFFICES were needed quickly in bomb-damaged areas. This house in Tresham Avenue, Homerton is doing duty as a fire guard point and food office about 1941.